Garlands for Mother

Compiled by

Ruth H. Wagner

Designed and illustrated by

Byron Barton

Published by The C. R. Gibson Company
Norwalk, Connecticut

Dedicated to the Memory of My Mother

Complete acknowledgments will be found in the back of the book.

TABLE OF CONTENTS

"Behold Thy Mother!"

Then saith he to the disciple, Behold thy mother! And from that hour that disciple took her unto his own home.

John 19: 27

"BEHOLD THY MOTHER!"

These words of Our Lord have for nineteen centuries ennobled that embodiment of heart and spirit which we know to be God's own handiwork — *the love of a mother*. There is an abiding faith in all deep love, but a mother's love is a veil of a softer light between the heart and the Heavenly Father.

Mary, the mother of Jesus, stood at the foot of the Cross and heard the coarse shouts of the crowd. Her Son then turned to John and bade him care for His beloved mother. "Even He that died for us upon the Cross, in the last hour, in the unutterable agony of death, was mindful of His mother, as if to teach us that this holy love should be our last worldly thought, the last point of earth from which the soul should take its flight to heaven" (Longfellow).

"Behold thy mother!"

ABIGAIL ADAMS

My mother was an angel upon earth. She was a minister of blessing to all human beings within her sphere of action. Her heart was the abode of heavenly purity. She had no feelings but of kindness and beneficence, yet her mind was as firm as her temper was mild and gentle. She had known sorrow, but her sorrow was silent . . . Had she lived to the age of the patriarchs, every day of her life would have been filled with clouds of goodness and of love.

John Quincy Adams

MY TRUST

A picture memory brings to me:
I look across the years and see
Myself beside my mother's knee.

I feel her gentle hand restrain
My selfish moods, and know again
A child's blind sense of wrong and pain.

But wiser now, a man gray grown,
My childhood's needs are better known,
My mother's chastening love I own.

John Greenleaf Whittier

Motherhood is, after all, woman's great and incomparable work.

Edward Carpenter

Whatever other things went wrong with me, the love of my true Mother never went wrong, but followed me ever inseparable, in good and evil fortune, and I should be harder of heart than would be suitable for man if I could ever forget that fact. And, alas, what can I do in return for you, dear Mother? Nothing, nothing! I will try to *live* by the noble example you showed; and to hold fast for myself, and speak abroad as I can, for others, the precious simple *wisdom* I learned from my Mother; let that be a comfort to her in her old age, in looking back upon a long life that has many sorrows in it.

Thomas Carlyle

Gramma Cutter

". . . when I was in my twenties," (Gramma) went on, "and the mother of two babies, we moved on again to the West. I've gathered my babies up to me and prayed that we'd get through the night without the Indians coming. I've lived in a sod house and shared the last of our family supplies with rough strangers. I've seen the grasshoppers take all our crops and a tornado lay every building low. I've seen the raw prairie with its long wild grass turn to mellow farm land and towns and cities. I've seen saplings grow to giant trees, and little boys to manhood." . . .

"With all this for the setting of our home life," the elderly woman continued, "we bore and brought up our children. We had our children work, not because we had theories that a little work is good for them, but because we had to eat to live, and it was absolute and sometimes cruel necessity that made every child have tasks to perform. For punishment, we couldn't keep their spending money from them; for, you see, none of us had any. We couldn't deny them much in the way of candy and sweets, for Christmas and Fourth of July were about the only times we had those things. The children worked hard and studied hard and played hard when there was time left over. And when they disobeyed they were punished. Someway, I never looked upon punishment as breaking the self-reliance of a child. I never dreamed that it was contrary to the best interest of the child mind. I thought of it as their first lesson in law and order and justice." . . .

"Eddie, now, he's a lawyer." Unconsciously (Gramma) was using the old childish names as she began the roll. "Sammie's on the old home-place, and has the best equipped farm for miles around. Joey's pastor of one of the largest churches in Minneapolis. Johnnie's on the faculty of the state university. He's studied at Oxford and written some text-books. Davy's on the staff of one of the Chicago hospitals. He specializes in abdominal surgery. And Bobbie, the rascaliest one of all, Bobbie's the new governor of the state where he was paddled."

Bess Streeter Aldrich

PIONEER MOTHER

She had no dream of empire, and no thought
Of heroism in her woman's share.
The triumphs that her hand and spirit wrought
Were slow-made things; she fashioned them to last
For others' use when her own days were passed.
She drew upon the quiet strength of prayer
To meet her needs, and with this strength
　　she fought
To build a home upon the conquered sod,
And bring her sons up worthy of their God.

Edna Casler Joll

Oh, wondrous power! how little understood,
　　Entrusted to the mother's mind alone,
To fashion genius, form the soul for good,
　　Inspire a West, or train a Washington.

Mrs. Sarah Josepha Hale

The Mother of George Washington

The mother of Washington, in forming him for those distinguished parts he was destined to perform, first taught him the duties of obedience, the better to prepare him for those of command. In the well-ordered domicile where his early years were passed, the levity and indulgence common to youth were tempered by a deference and well-regulated restraint which, while it curtailed no rational enjoyment usual in the spring-time of life, prescribed those enjoyments within the bounds of moderation and propriety.

The matron held in reserve an authority which never departed from her, not even when her son had become the most illustrious of men. It seemed to say, 'I am your mother, the being who gave you life, the guide who directed your steps when they needed the guidance of age and wisdom, the parental affection which claimed your love, the parental authority which commanded your obedience; whatever may be your success, whatever your renown, next to your God you owe most to me.' Nor did the chief dissent from these truths, but to the last moment of the life of his venerable parent, he yielded to her will the most dutiful, implicit obedience, and felt for her person and character the most holy reverence and attachment.

George Washington Parke Custis

One lamp, thy mother's love, amid the stars shall lift its pure flame changeless, and before the throne of God burn through eternity.

A. P. Willis

THE BOOK OUR MOTHERS READ

We search the world for truth; we cull
The good, the pure, the beautiful,
From graven stone and written scroll,
And all old flower-fields of the soul;
And, weary seekers of the best,
We come back laden from the quest,
To find that all the sages said
Is in the Book our mothers read.

John Greenleaf Whittier

Give me the life of the boy whose mother is nurse, seamstress, washerwoman, cook, teacher, angel, and saint, all in one, and whose father is guide, exemplar, and friend. No servants to come between. These are the boys who are born to the best fortune.

Andrew Carnegie

And while with care our mother laid
The work aside, her steps she stayed
One moment, seeking to express
Her grateful sense of happiness
For food and shelter, warmth and health,
And love's contentment more than wealth,
With simple wishes (not the weak
Vain prayers which no fulfillment seek,
But such as warm the generous heart,
O'er-prompt to do with Heaven its part)
That none might lack, that bitter night,
For bread and clothing, warmth and light.

John Greenleaf Whittier

God made mothers before He made ministers;
the progress of Christ's kingdom depends more
upon the influence of faithful, wise, and pious
mothers than upon any other human agency.

T. L. Cuyler

MOTHER'S LAUGHTER

Mother's laughter, which was laughter with all
the silver bells ringing, seemed to be an outward
expression of the determination in her character.
She *would* raise us so that we turned out at our
best. Father's salary, when I first became aware
of such things, was four hundred dollars a year.
I remember my sense of affluence when it rose to
six hundred: I wondered what we would do with
the extra money. It was Mother with her flying
hands and fighting heart, who supplemented the
income and held us together. We were never for-
saken and we never begged, but we were undeni-
ably outfitted from missionary boxes that came
from the more affluent churches of the East. Some
of the contents of those boxes were wonderful and
others were not — garments frayed and faded,
shoes without mates, games that lacked parts or
directions, dolls that were losing their sawdust.
Mother had all the answers. As she once remarked,
she "died" with every dress she "dyed" and then
made over. She invented new rules for the games;
she stuffed the limp dolls; she converted the lonely
shoes into sandals. I never owned an overcoat until
I was in high school, and then one green with age
came in a box. It fit me, and Mother dyed it . . .

Mother did something that was even more wonderful — she raised her "p. k.'s," her preacher's kids, without letting them develop inferiority complexes. Not one of us, such was her inspired way, ever had the slightest idea that he was unfortunate or to be pitied. We were taught to pray for wisdom and guidance, for direct help in practical, everyday matters. The example our parents gave us was, perhaps, a childlike faith, but never did those prayers for Heaven's aid conclude without the acceptance of responsibility for getting busy. "Pray without ceasing and work accordingly" was one of Father's mottoes, and one of his favorite texts was, "Faith without works is dead."

Daniel A. Poling

All that is purest and best in man is but the echo of a mother's benediction. The hero's deeds are but a mother's prayers fulfilled.

Frederic W. Morton

The harshness and general painfulness of life in old times must have been much relieved by certain simple and affectionate customs which modern people have learned to dispense with. Amongst these was a practice of going to see parents, and especially the female one, on the mid Sunday of Lent, taking for them some little present, such as a cake or a trinket. A youth engaged in this amiable act of duty was said to go *a-mothering*, and thence the day itself came to be called Mothering Sunday.

Chambers Book of Days

What are Raphael's Madonnas but the shadow
of a mother's love, fixed in permanent outline forever?

Thomas W. Higginson

A mother is a mother still,
The holiest thing alive.

Samuel Taylor Coleridge

In the second century before Christ there was
a Roman lady well adorned with jewels who called
on Cornelia, the mother of two boys who after-
wards became immensely famous as the Gracchi.
The visitor, noticing that Cornelia had no jewels
on her person, asked, "Where are your jewels?"
Cornelia sent for the two little boys and said,
"These are my jewels" — four words which are
among the most famous ever spoken.

From Seneca

Oh, fair young mother! On thy brow
Shall sit a nobler grace than now.
Deep in the brightness of the skies
The thronging years in glory rise,
   And, as they fleet,
Drop strength and riches at thy feet.

William Cullen Bryant

As one whom his mother comforteth, so will I
comfort you.

Isaiah 66 : 13

Mother, there is a love
Men give to wives and children, lovers, friends;
There is a love which some men give to God.
Ah! between this, I think, and that last love,
Last and too-late-discovered love of God,
There shines — and nearer to the love of God —
The love a man gives only to his mother,
Whose travail of dear thought has never end
Until the End.

John Freeman

A mother's love, the best love; **God's** love, the highest love.

From the German

What the mother sings to the cradle goes all the way down to the grave.

Henry Ward Beecher

God could not be everywhere, and therefore he made mothers.

Jewish Proverb

When Eve was brought unto Adam, he became filled with the Holy Spirit, and gave her the most sanctified, the most glorious of appellations. He called her Eva, that is to say, the Mother of All. He did not style her wife, but simply mother — mother of all living creatures. In this consists the glory and the most precious ornament of women.

Martin Luther

There are teachings in earth, and sky, and air,
The heavens the glory of God declare;
But louder than voice, beneath, above,
He is heard to speak through a mother's love.

Emily Taylor

IDA STOVER EISENHOWER

Even though Mrs. Eisenhower was an exceedingly strong character, with fixed ideas about what was right and wrong, she was the wisest of mothers in that she determined not to interfere with her sons' choice of careers. It is a strange quirk of destiny that one of her sons should decide to go to West Point. When Ike ran home from his entrance examination his mother saw him coming across the vacant lot. She rushed upstairs to her own room for a split second of sorrow. Her faith almost failed her. Then she heard his joyous cry, "Mother! Mother! Mother! Where are you? I made it!" The mother brushed away the tears and descended the steps, calm and serene. "It's splendid, son. I knew you would."

Even though it seemed almost like blasphemy for a son of hers to become a warrior, she reasoned it must be the will of God. Her hatred of war remained intense. She had often told him that "those who lived by the sword would perish by it." In fact, the General says that she was never a "meek" pacifist. "She probably prayed secretly that I would fail my examinations." She had such confidence in Dwight's character, she knew it must be right, although beyond her comprehension.

As the Supreme Commander stood on the beach before the rocky cliffs of Malta, he thought, "Tomorrow they will land . . . Will the Allies win, will many precious boys lose their lives?" He had to have help from a source higher than himself. "Is my decision to land troops on Sicily justified?" He bent his knees on the sand and prayed. Again on "D Day", in June 1944, under the weight of his final decision to cross the English Channel, he went alone to his quarters. His mother's life and teachings had not been in vain.

Elizabeth Logan Davis

A Mother's Name

No painter's brush, nor poet's pen
   In justice to her fame
Has ever reached half high enough
   To write a mother's name.

December, 1861

A quiet Christmas; no presents but apples and flowers. No merrymaking; for Nan and Mary were gone and Betty under the snow. But we are used to hard times, and, as mother says, "While there is a famine in Kansas, we mustn't ask for sugar-plums."

All the philosophy in our house is not in the study; a good deal of it is in the kitchen, where a fine old lady thinks high thoughts and does kind deeds while she cooks and scrubs.

Louisa May Alcott

INAUGURATION DAY

When the oath of office had been administered, and President James A. Garfield had reverently kissed the Bible and sealed his compact with the nation to rightly administer its law for the term for which he was chosen, when thousands of eyes rested upon him to see the next act in the drama being enacted, in the presence of the foreign dignitaries and leading men of the country, he turned to his aged mother, who had been unconsciously weeping during the delivery of his address, and kissed her; then he kissed his wife — the two persons of all the world most interested with him in the events they had witnessed.

The act, the most unexpected at that moment, called forth cheers from the multitude who witnessed it, and the one incident of the inauguration that most impressed upon all who saw it was the tribute paid to his mother and wife by the President. Wherever the soldiers wandered in Washington during that day, wherever the news was flashed over the wires to the distant sections of our own country or to foreign lands, was heard this sentence: "The President kissed his mother."

Laura C. Holloway

There never was a woman like her. She was gentle as a dove and brave as a lioness . . . The memory of my mother and her teachings were after all the only capital I had to start life with, and on that capital I have made my way.

Andrew Jackson

DEFINITION

I search among the plain and lovely words
To find what one word "Mother" means; as well
Try to define the tangled song of birds;
The echo in the hills of one clear bell.
One cannot snare the wind, or catch the wings
Of shadows flying low across the wheat;
Ah, who can prison simple, natural things
That make the long days beautiful and sweet?

Mother — a word that holds the tender spell
Of all the dear essential things of earth;
A home, clean sunlit rooms, and the good smell
Of bread; a table spread; a glowing hearth.
And love beyond the dream of anyone . . .
I search for words for her . . . and there are none.

Grace Noll Crowell

The sweetest sounds to mortals given
Are heard in Mother, Home, and Heaven.

William Goldsmith Brown

THE GIFT

God thought to give the sweetest thing
   In His almighty power
To earth; and deeply pondering
   What it should be — one hour
In fondest joy and love of heart
   Outweighing every other,
He moved the gates of heaven apart
   And gave to earth — a Mother!

G. Newell Lovejoy

Who ran to help me when I fell
And would some pretty story tell,
Or kiss the place to make it well?
My mother.

Ann Taylor

A mother's smile is one of the wonders of nature.

WHAT IS A MOTHER?

If there is something one cannot do without, it is Mother. Father loves her, daughter imitates her, son ignores her, salesmen thrive on her, motorists hurry around her, teacher phones her, and the woman next door confides in her.

She can be sweeter than sugar, more sour than a lemon, all smiles, and crying her heart out all within any given two-minute period.

She likes sewing, detective stories, having her birthday remembered, church, a new dress, the cleaning woman, Father's praise, a little lipstick, flowers and plants, canasta, dinner out on Sunday, policemen, one whole day in bed, crossword puzzles, sunny days, tea, and the newspaper boy.

She dislikes doing the dishes, Father's boss, having her birthday forgotten, the motorist behind her, spring cleaning, Junior's report card, rainy days, the neighbors' dog, stairs, and the man who was supposed to cut the grass.

She can be found standing by, bending over, reaching for, kneeling under, and stretching around, but rarely sitting on.

She has the beauty of a spring day, the patience of a saint, the appetite of a small bird, and the memory of a large elephant.

She knows the lowest prices, everybody's birthday, what you should be doing, and all your secret thoughts.

She is always straightening up after, reminding you to, and taking care of, but never asking for.

Yes, a Mother is one thing that nobody can do without. And when you have harassed her, buffeted her about, tried her patience, and worn her out, and it seems that the end of the world is about to descend upon you, then you can win her back with four little words, "Mom, I love you!"

William A. Greenebaum II

WONDROUS MOTHERHOOD

Thank God! for that lovely spirit
That makes motherhood akin.

They have known the way of travail.
They have known the pangs of pain.
They have compassed hope and sorrow.
They have had both tears and joy.
That is why a glowing radiance
Shines in all they say and do.

That is why they are the blessed,
Why we hail them far and wide
Dearest of all God's creations,
Great and wondrous motherhood.

A Son's Care

At the hour when the other school-boys went to play, (Robert E. Lee) hurried home to order his mother's drive, and would then be seen carrying her in his arms to the carriage and arranging her cushions with the gentleness of an experienced nurse. One of his relatives . . . tells of the exertions he would make on these occasions to entertain and amuse his mother; assuring her, with the gravity of an old man, that unless she was cheerful the drive would not benefit her. When she complained of cold or drafts, he would pull from his pocket a great jack-knife and newspaper and make her laugh with his efforts to improvise curtains and shut out the intrusive wind which whistled through the crevices of the old family coach.

When he left her to go to West Point his mother was heard to say, "How can I live without Robert? He is both son and daughter to me."

Stanley F. Horn

I think it must somewhere be written, that the virtues of mothers shall be visited on their children, as well as the sins of their fathers.

Charles Dickens

My mother was the making of me. She was so true and so sure of me I felt I had something to live for — someone I must not disappoint. The memory of my mother will always be a blessing to me.

Thomas A. Edison

LOUISE ABIGAIL MAYO

Mother Louise and the Mayo boys climbed to the tower on top of their farm house, where, with her own inventive hands, she had put together the four-foot telescope and fastened it on a tripod. Mother Louise always climbed with the inquiring Mayo sons to show them the pattern of the stars. Later, when the elder son, Dr. Will, built his own house, his one request was that it include "a tower like the one from which I watched the stars with mother." In fact, the world-renowned Mayo doctors, Dr. Will and Dr. Charlie, when asked about their success, repeatedly told their biographers, "We were born of the right parents at the right time."

Elizabeth Logan Davis

The memories that have come to me today of my mother who was born here are very affecting, and her quiet character, her sense of duty and dislike of affectation, have come back to me with increasing force as those years of duty have accumulated. Yet perhaps it is appropriate that in a place of worship I should acknowledge my indebtedness to her and to her remarkable father, because, after all, what the world is now seeking to do is to return to the paths of duty, to turn away from the savagery of interest to the dignity of the performance of right.

Woodrow Wilson
On the occasion of his visit on December 29, 1918, to his grandfather's church — Lowther Street Congregational Church, Carlisle, England.

Our Hearts Were Young and Gay

I tried to bid my parents a worldly, indifferent good-bye but it was hard to get away with. Mother, despite my 19 years and a lamentable determination to look like Theda Bara, the "vamp" of the movies in that era, still persisted in calling me "Baby." She kept reminding me to put my purse in my pillow, never to speak to any strange men, always to spread paper on "the seat," and to write if I arrived safely. This was my first flight from the home nest; Mother cried a little and Father looked as if he never expected to meet me again. This despite the fact that they too were sailing for England, although on a different ship. They had no idea of cramping our style but they thought it just as well to be in the same hemisphere as we.

Montreal was my first experience of registering alone at a hotel, and far from feeling emancipated and like Theda Bara, I felt frightened and forlorn. I was too shy to venture forth alone in a strange town, and was afraid of not being on hand when Emily (Kimbrough) arrived. I wrote letters, studied bits of Baedeker, and every 15 minutes made certain my passport and letter of credit hadn't been stolen.

This last activity involved opening up a humiliating little contraption that Mother had harnessed about my person. It was an incredible object known as a "safety-pocket," a large chamois purse that dangled at the knees in the manner of a Scot's sporran and was attached to an adjustable belt around the waist. It was supposed to be worn inconspicuously under skirt and slip. I daresay in Mother's youthful and voluminously clad day it could thus be concealed, and nobody was the wiser. But in my more skimpy day, everybody was not only the wiser but the more bewildered. The bag was heavily stuffed with British bank notes, my passport and letter of credit. When I walked it would swing, catching between my knees and making me go into a gait of an animated ice-hook. When I sat still it had an unfortunate way of coming to rest along my outer thigh, giving me the outline of someone concealing a squash.

At long last Emily arrived, and the sounds of our greeting made ring whatever the welkin is. At bedtime that night in the hotel room which we shared, the moment was at hand when Emily would see me attired only in that safety-pocket, and I thought it wise to prepare her. "Emily," I began, "I must tell you . . . I have to . . . to wear something —"

She cut me short. "Stop!" she cried. "I've been wondering for days how to tell *you*." With a dramatic gesture she swished up her skirt and there, dangling between her legs like a gourd from a vine, was the twin of my ghastly safety-pocket. "Mother made me wear one too," she groaned.

Cornelia Otis Skinner

Take a vine of a good soil,
And the daughter of a good mother.

Italian Proverb

I'm for Mother's Day!

With the figure of a model, the mind of an intellectual and the heart of a rebel, my mother grew into adulthood fifty years too soon. The restrictions of her time imprisoned her in a ladylike world she was too well-brought-up to ignore. When she was young, dancing was slightly naughty, working girls, unladylike. Boys must be demurely waited for, an exposed ankle was nakedness. She adventured when she could — climbed mountains in boyish puttees, bathed in frightful, flapping bloomers, played tennis on the lawn, and once, she says musingly, "I kissed a boy on the beach."

I can imagine it. Not much can intimidate Mother. It was a cruel quirk of fate that she, loving men from baby boys to grandfathers, should have been widowed so early. My brother and I thought a new father would be a good idea, but though she loved men she loved her children more, and the man didn't come along whom she deemed fit to be our father.

Her comfortable, decorous bringing up had left her completely unequipped technically to make a living. Spurning training for a nine-to-five job which would keep her away from us too long, she turned her interest in people into a financial asset. She sold everything from homemade marmalade to knitted suits and brought us triumphantly through the depression, and helped my brother in his long struggle through the university.

I've watched her charm her way to the heart of the surliest bus driver. I've known her to push a watermelon home with her foot because her arms were filled with parcels.

I was with her the winter when, with white hair and dimming eyes, she made her first trip on a chair lift, 4000 feet up a mountain, flirting outrageously with the operators at each end of the ride and wishing aloud for a pair of snowshoes as she plodded through the deep snow. Some of my contemporaries fret over a plane trip but Mother flies by jet, loving it, and marvelling at the tremendous efficiency of "those dear boys up front."

She'll hang out my wash, make a batch of sour milk cookies because they are her grandchildren's favorites, put a new pocket in an old pair of jeans, listen with delight to her oldest grandson's romance, and with sympathy to anyone's troubles, crisply correct any grammatical mistakes we might be imprudent enough to make, and then remark woefully, "I just can't do anything more."

She's fiercely opposed to smoking, but, for her generation, tolerant about sex. When we tease her about it, she says indignantly "sex is much more natural." Recently she had an eye operation, and she was the darling of the ward because not one day during the five weeks of her sightlessness did she neglect her lipstick. And not one romance among the nurses did she leave uncovered.

I think Mother knows that these are among the qualities we love in her. But I know we don't tell her so often enough. Ideally, we should show our appreciation every day. But we're too busy, too thoughtless, too inarticulate, or just too shy. For such reasons I think Mother's Day is justified.

Lois Light

How We Kept Mother's Day

One year our family decided to have a special celebration of Mother's Day, as a token of appreciation for all the sacrifices that Mother had made for us. After breakfast we had arranged, as a surprise, to hire a car and take her for a beautiful drive in the country. Mother was rarely able to have a treat like that, because she was busy in the house nearly all the time.

But on the very morning of the day, we changed the plan a little, because it occurred to Father that it would be even better to take Mother fishing. As the car was hired and paid for, we might just as well use it to drive up into the hills where the streams are. As Father said, if you just go out driving, you have a sense of aimlessness, but if you are going to fish, there is a definite purpose that heightens the enjoyment.

So we all felt it would be nicer for Mother to have a definite purpose; and anyway, Father had just got a new rod the day before, which he said Mother could use if she wanted to; only Mother said she would much rather watch him fish than try to fish herself.

So we got her to make up a sandwich lunch in case we got hungry, though of course we were to come home again to a big festive dinner.

Well, when the car came to the door, it turned out that there wasn't as much room in it as we had supposed, because we hadn't reckoned on Father's fishing gear and the lunch, and it was plain that we couldn't all get in.

Father said not to mind him, that he could just as well stay home and put in the time working in the garden. He said that we were not to let the fact that he had not had a real holiday for three years stand in our way; he wanted us to go right ahead and have a big day and not to mind him.

But of course we all felt that it would never do to let Father stay home, especially as we knew he would make trouble if he did. The two girls, Anna and Mary, would have stayed and gotten dinner, only it seemed such a pity to, on a lovely day like this, since they had their new hats. But they said that Mother had only to say the word and they'd gladly stay home and work. Will and I would have dropped out, but we wouldn't have been any use in getting the dinner.

So in the end it was decided that Mother would stay home and just have a lovely restful day around the house, and get the dinner. Also it turned out to be just a bit raw out-of-doors, and Father said he would never forgive himself if he dragged Mother round the country and let her take a severe cold. He said it was our duty to let Mother get all the rest and quiet she could, after all she had done for all of us, and that young people seldom realize how much quiet means to people who are getting old. He could still stand the racket, but he was glad to shelter Mother from it.

Well, we had the loveliest day up among the hills, and Father caught such big specimens that he felt sure that Mother couldn't have landed them anyway, if she had been fishing for them. Will and I fished, too, and the two girls met some young men friends along the stream, and so we all had a splendid time.

It was quite late when we got back, but Mother had guessed that we would be late, so she had kept back the dinner to have it hot for us.

We sat down to a big roast turkey. Mother had to get up and down a good bit during the meal fetching things, but at the end Father noticed it and said she simply mustn't do it, that he wanted her to spare herself, and he got up and fetched the walnuts from the sideboard himself.

The dinner was great fun, and when it was over all of us wanted to help clear the things up and wash the dishes, only Mother said that she would really much rather do it, and so we let her, because we wanted to humor her.

It was late when it was all over, and when we kissed Mother before going to bed, she said it had been the most wonderful day in her life, and I think there were tears in her eyes.

Stephen Leacock

A mother is not a person to lean on but a person to make leaning unnecessary.

Dorothy Canfield Fisher

Most of all the other beautiful things in life come by twos and threes, by dozens and hundreds. Plenty of roses, stars, sunsets, rainbows, brothers and sisters, aunts and cousins, but only one *mother* in the whole world.

Kate Douglas Wiggin

Youth fades; love droops; the heavens of
   friendship fall;
A Mother's secret hope outlives them all.

Oliver Wendell Holmes

My mother was as mild as any saint,
And nearly canonized by all she knew,
So gracious was her tact and tenderness.

Alfred, Lord Tennyson

No language can express the power and beauty
and heroism and majesty of a mother's love. It
shrinks not where man cowers, and grows stronger
where man faints, and over the wastes of worldly
fortune sends the radiance of its quenchless
fidelity like a star in heaven.

E. H. Chapin

The love of a mother is never exhausted, it
never changes, it never tires. A father may turn
his back on his child, brothers and sisters may
become inveterate enemies, husbands may desert
their wives, wives their husbands, but a mother's
love endures through all; in good repute, in bad
repute, in the face of the world's condemnation,
a mother still loves on, and still hopes that her
child may turn from his evil ways and repent;
still she remembers the infant smiles that once
filled her bosom with rapture, the merry laugh,
the joyful shout of his childhood, the opening
promise of his youth; and she can never be brought
to think him all unworthy.

Washington Irving

MOTHER'S WAY OF RESTING

I often marvel why it was I gave so little thought
To all the helpful lessons which my patient
    mother taught.
Now older grown, and she has gone, I often
    long to tell
Her how they all come back to me, each one
    remembered well.
For in the work and cares of life that come
    from day to day,
I find I stop to ask myself, "What was my
    mother's way?"

There never seemed to be with her a drudgery
    of life;
She got along so quietly with all its cares and
    strife.
She always sang about her work, and 'mid
    perplexing things
The farmhouse walls re-echoed, "Rise, my soul,
    and stretch thy wings."
I never hear old "Amsterdam" but that I think
    how oft
It bore my mother's soul from earth to unseen
    things aloft.

When sitting in her rocking chair, her lap with
    mending piled,
She used to say, "I want to rest, now read a
    Psalm, my child."
I learned by heart about "the hills" and "lifting
    up my eyes";
Those "pastures green" and "waters still"
    the Shepherd's love supplies;
And all about "abiding 'neath the shadow of
    His wing";
For "God our refuge is our strength" I read
    in everything.

Sometimes I hurried through the Psalm, taking
    but little heed,
And then her thanks, so kindly said, encouraged
    me to read
Some of the words that Jesus spoke, for that
    was mother's way —
To read from Psalms and Gospels both upon
    the busiest day;
For at such times she needed a much longer
    rest, and so
While but a child, I learned her favorite
    passages to know.

Those precious words of quiet come to my own
    soul, now I
A busy woman, full of work, my daily duties ply.
I sing her hymns when fretted with my ceaseless
    rounds of care;
I repeat the Psalms and Gospels when in my
    sewing chair.
I wonder if she knows it, and how glad I am
    each day
That my mother's way of resting was such
    a helpful way.

Susan Teall Perry

Of all the men I have known, I cannot recall
one whose mother did her level best for him when
he was little who did not turn out well when he
grew up.

Frances Parkinson Keyes

There is none,
In all this cold and hollow world, no fount
Of deep, strong, deathless love, save that within
A mother's heart.

Felicia D. Hemans

MOTHER AND HER SECRET

You hear a lot about kids fooling their mothers, but you hardly ever hear of a mother fooling her kids. But I knew one who did. Mine. But in the end we found out the truth about her.

We grew up during the Depression. Now kids today may not know what a depression means. It doesn't mean one car in the family and steak once a week, even if that is as ghastly a life as kids today can imagine. The Depression meant no shoes, no meat and barely enough shelter — with a fighting chance that the whole family would be evicted onto the sidewalk. That was the Depression. And it was harder still because our father had left us.

Well, all through those grim years my mother managed to keep her four children fed, sheltered, clothed, and in school. Her hair turned white before she was 35. She was cheerful enough, but her eyes had a sort of haunted look. She never had any pretty clothes or good times.

When we four kids grew up, we all did well enough to pool a fairly handsome hunk of cash to send Mom each week, so that whatever years she had left from about 50 on would be different from the years before. But we were all kind of disappointed in Mom's new life. She didn't move into a new home; she said she was perfectly comfortable in the old one. She didn't hire any help to take her off her feet; she said she liked doing housework. She didn't buy any pretty clothes. She kept delaying the vacations to Florida or to Europe that we planned for her — until we gave up planning. Still, that weekly check came in, and, as we four figured it, since she didn't spend more than a fraction of it each week she must have saved a considerable amount by the time she died, some 20 years later.

Well, when we went through her papers we found that Mom was broke! Those checks had been spent the instant they arrived. On what? As soon as we kids were off her back, Mom had secretly arranged with a refugee outfit to ship her four war orphans from Europe. She'd set them up in a home near hers, and for 20 years she'd educated them, seen them through sickness and teen-age problems, and, in two cases, into marriage.

She never told us about the four new kids. I guess she wasn't sure we'd approve of her going through the whole mess all over again. I'm not sure we would have, either. You see, it isn't easy for kids who've grown up seeing their mothers knock themselves out half their lives to raise them to understand that motherhood is a sort of incurable condition.

Al Capp

Every man is privileged to believe all his life that his own mother is the best and dearest that a child ever had. By some strange racial instinct of taciturnity and repression most of us lack utterance to say our thoughts in this close matter. A man's mother is so tissued and woven into his life and brain that he can no more describe her than describe the air and sunlight that bless his days.

Christopher Morley

LETTER TO A BRIDE AND GROOM

Tuesday, November 30, 1934

My precious Children:

Thinking of you, loving you, dreaming of a radiant future for you, I someway find it difficult to express the depth and tenderness of my feelings. Often I have felt the utter futility of words; never more than now when I would wish my boy and his bride the highest and truest happiness together. That I love you and that my fondest hopes are centered in you, I do not need to assure you, my own dear children.

My dear Bird, I earnestly hope that you will love me as I do you. Lyndon has always held a very special place in my heart. Will you not share that place with him, dear child? It would make me very happy to have you for my very own, to have you turn to me with love and confidence, to let me mother you as I do my precious boy. My heart is full of earnest wishes for your happiness. From a mother's standpoint however I can scarcely say more than this. I hope, and hope you know is composed of desire and expectation, that Lyndon will prove to be as tender, as true, as loyal, as loving, and as faithful a husband as he has been a son. May life's richest blessings be yours, dear little girl.

My darling boy, I rejoice in your happiness, the happiness you so richly deserve, the fruition of the hopes of early manhood, the foundation of a completely rounded life. I have always desired the best in life for you. Now, that you have the love and companionship of the one and only girl, I am sure you will go far. You are fortunate in finding and winning the girl you love, and I am sure your love for each other will be an incentive to you to do all the great things of which you are capable. Sweet son, I am loving you and counting on you as never before.

Now, my beloved children, I shall be longing to see you soon. Write me. Enjoy your honeymoon in that ideal setting then hurry home to see us.

My dearest love to you both,

Mamma

Rebekah Baines Johnson

All great mothers have been created by their sons or their daughters.
G. Bromley Oxenham

All that I am or hope to be, I owe to my angel mother.
Abraham Lincoln

No man is poor who has had a Godly mother.

Abraham Lincoln

Mighty is the force of motherhood! It transforms all things by its vital heat.
George Eliot

"Like mother, like son" is a saying so true
The world will judge largely the "mother" by you.

Margaret Johnston Grafflin

Mary Hatten White

When I began to talk about bringing Sallie
Lindsay over for dinner, my mother became all
fluttered about a plain, black walnut rocking chair
with the simplest lines, almost crude. And she
began hunting downtown for a covering, and up-
holstered it herself and wrapped it so heavily that
it was hard for anyone to squeeze into it. This
was done for Sallie Lindsay. It was the only piece
of furniture that my father had brought from his
home in Ohio. His mother, Fear Perry, had had
it at her marriage in Lee, Massachusetts, to my
grandfather, John White. My mother liked to believe that his mother, Martha Keith, had rocked
him in that old chair as a child during the Revolu-
tion. Certainly Fear Perry had used it. My father
and Mary Hatten had rocked me in it, and I think
my mother, with that feminine instinct for breed-
ing which makes a woman yearn in the spring to
set a hen, had some designs on Sallie Lindsay and
her son with that old walnut chair. We still have
it in an honored place in our house, and my
mother's son's son's wife may use it for her child
some day. Anyway, I watched the little byplay
of my mother fussing with that chair. I tried to
dissuade her, but she was set on it; and, to avoid
a spat, I let her have her hour of romance, lining
the nest, even if the lining made the nest unin-
habitable.

Of course my mother was jealous of Sallie
Lindsay. She had even looked with a baleful eye
on Alice Murdock, the little cripple whom I had
grown up with as a sister. Any girl at whom I
looked twice ruffled her feathers. But she tried
to be sweet about Sallie Lindsay, knowing probably that I had come into the zone when men mar-

ried. So she scrubbed, dusted, swept, burnished and pushed the furniture around for days before the visit, and I believe she was happy. Her indomitable energy was finding an outlet for her inner fear, and maybe unconscious rage, at losing the apple of her eye, the one thing she had to show for a dream of romance that was always a bit drab and had not quite come true. She accepted the inevitable probably, but with reservations. She was determined in her heart to show Sallie Lindsay the schoolteacher that she, Mary Hatten the schoolteacher, was "folks," somebody — the wife of Dr. Allen White who died mayor of Eldorado. So when Sallie Lindsay crossed her threshold, my mother was determined that this young lady should meet a paragon of Yankee housekeeping. Above all, she wanted to flaunt her cooking.

So I bought a thick beefsteak. We had soup with brown barley in it made from the recipe which I had brought back from the Midland Hotel. It was our show piece. Sallie, who was only twenty-one, was shy, and my mother and I were most circumspect. It was a trying but happy hour, I think, for all of us.

William Allen White

Dear Mom,

You are one of the world's hardest gals to please on Mother's Day.

The ordinary presents are no good at all. You don't want jewelry. If your children buy you candy or flowers, you say, "It's just a waste of money." They can't give you money with any sense of satisfaction because they know you won't spend it on yourself. You'll just put it away in an old sock for your grandchildren.

"Oh, don't give me anything — Mother's Day is just a bunch of nonsense," you say. Your happiest Mother's Days have been the ones on which you spent five hours burning your face cherry red over a cookstove fixing a family feast — in the years when the whole family could be there to enjoy it.

What could one who was away do to please you except to call you long-distance and tell you he missed you and wished he was home? It is hard to give anything to a woman who has spent her life in giving to others.

The only thing I have to offer you is the one thing you never asked for — appreciation.

Why do I love you? Let me count the reasons — just a few:

I love you because you are my mother, not only of my body but of my spirit's hunger.

I love you because when I deserved and needed a switching, I got it — not later, but right then when I knew I had done wrong, felt guilty, and recognized I should be punished.

I love you because you never let tomorrow's sun rise on yesterday's anger.

I love you because you played no favorites among your children. Your only favorite child (this is still true) was the one that most needed your understanding help at the time.

I love you because when the cat had too many kittens you couldn't bear to have them drowned. (With five kids yourself you could understand the mother cat's problem.)

I love you because, although you only had a third-grade education, you never ceased reading and learning and widening the horizon of your own mind. And from your mind my mind caught fire.

I love you because you always watered and fed my adolescent dreams.

I love you because, when Dad died nearly 19 years ago, you refused to turn into a self-pitying widow. Time has mellowed you. It cannot shrivel or defeat you.

I love you because, now that your children have grown, you refuse to try to run their lives. You merely say mildly, "Learn to sit loosely in the saddle of life."

I love you because, although you and I have always felt free to talk to each other about anything, from the whims of God to the frailties of man, I feel I really know less about you than almost anyone I know at all. You have always held a mystery to me, you always will. The more you love people, the more you realize there is a part of them you cannot ever know.

Finally, I love you because I know that when you read this you will be embarrassed and say, "Now, why did he have to do that? Can't he think of something more important to write about than that?"

Well, not today, Mom.

Respectfully,
Your long son,
Harold

Hal Boyle

WHAT IS A MOTHER?

A mother is a person who is old enough to be an authority on Indian war whoops and whether cowboys ever went barefoot, and yet young enough to remember the rules of the game May I? and the second verse of Sing a Song of Sixpence.

She must be smart enough to answer questions about thunder and locomotives and stars, but ignorant enough to laugh at the reason a chicken runs across the road.

She must be a detective and able to find the top to the cereal box which was thrown away last week, the treads to Greg's toy tank, and the other roller skate.

She must be a veterinarian and accomplished at taking ticks off the dog, feeding the kittens, and remembering to change the water in the goldfish bowl.

A mother must not just be a cook, proficient at cooking roasts, biscuits, chicken gravy, Mike's favorite sukiyaki and Greg's favorite spaghetti; but also must be able to decorate birthday cakes and place exactly right the raisin eyes in gingerbread men.

She must be a judge and arbitrator when someone would not let someone ride his tricycle; must be a stern disciplinarian when it comes to too much chewing gum and getting three little boys to bed at night; and she must have a well-padded shoulder for tears and comfort when his best chum throws sand at Mike and goes off with a new friend.

She must not only be an expert laundress, but always remember to remove sand and pebbles and string from pockets; and she must be a seamstress and adept at sewing on buttons, letting down and taking up sleeves and pants legs and able to patch threadbare corduroy knees so the patches do not show.

She must be a doctor and able to remove splinters without hurting, stop bleeding noses, vaporize colds, read stories to measle-speckled boys, and always have on hand an endless supply of ready-cut bandages.

A mother must also be a naturalist and able to dissect caterpillars, remove taillights from fireflies, and touch squirmy worms.

A mother must be a financial wizard and always able to stretch a meager weekly budget to include new shoes for Brian and a birthday present for someone she did not know had invited her sons to a party.

She must be a magician and keep a bottomless cooky jar, a constant supply of apples in the refrigerator, and be able instantly to recognize a scribbled drawing as a beautiful picture of a man walking down a dirt road with a pan on his head.

She must be able to balance a baby under one arm, a small boy climbing up her back and another trying to tie her feet into knots, and still write a check for the dry cleaners.

Regardless of her shape or stature, when she sits down a mother must have a lap large enough to hold three wiggling pajama-clad boys who listen wonder-eyed to "Once upon a time" stories of the world about them.

Her sense of beauty must be able to stoop low enough to see the lovely ferny plant Greg found growing under a toadstool; and must be able to stretch on tallest tiptoes to hold Mike to see the heavenly blue of the robin's egg in the nest in the sycamore tree.

A mother is a queer sort of person. In a single instant her endless cooking and dishwashing and ironing and sock darning and knee bandaging can swell over into a heart-thrilling wave of pride on visitors' day at the kindergarten when Mike stands up in his new red sweater, replies "Yes, ma'am" to the teacher, and solemnly walks to the front of the room to direct the rhythm band.

A mother's payment is rich and full, but often comes in little ways: a wadded bouquet of dandelion puffs; seeing Greg, unnoticed, share his tricycle with the new little boy across the street; watching Brian reach to pluck a neighbor's prize tulip . . . hold his hand in mid-air a second . . . and then toddle off to chase a butterfly. Her payment comes in the cherished words of a small boy's prayers at night when Mike adds a P. S. to God to "also bless Billy even though he pushed me off the swing today."

Then a mother kisses three blond heads, turns off the light and hugs a smile to her heart as she walks downstairs. And after the dishes are done, before she gets out her mending box, she puts a batch of cookies in the oven for a surprise tomorrow.

Nan Carroll

Nobody Knows but Mother

How many buttons are missing today?
How many playthings are strewn in her way?
    Nobody knows but mother.
How many thimbles and spools has she missed?
How many burns on each little fist?
How many bumps to be cuddled and kissed?
    Nobody knows but mother.

How many stockings to darn, do you know?
How many muddy shoes all in a row?
    Nobody knows but mother.
How many little torn aprons to mend?
How many hours of toil must she spend?
What is the time when her day's work shall end?
    Nobody knows but mother.

How many cares does a mother-heart know?
How many joys from her mother-love flow?
    Nobody knows but mother.
How many prayers by each little white bed?
How many tears for her babe has she shed?
How many kisses for each curly head?
    Nobody knows but mother.

Mary Morrison

A mother's love for the child of her body differs
essentially from all other affections, and burns
with so steady and clear a flame that it appears
like the one unchangeable thing in this earthly
mutable life, so that when she is no longer present
it is still a light to our steps and a consolation.

W. H. Hudson

The real religion of the world comes from women much more than from men — from mothers most of all, who carry the key of our souls in their bosoms.

Oliver Wendell Holmes

They talk about a woman's sphere as though it
   had a limit —
There's not a place in earth or heaven
There's not a place to mankind given
There's not a blessing or a woe
There's not a whispered yes or no
There's not a life or death or birth
There's not a feather's weight of worth
Without a woman in it.

Woman is the salvation or destruction of the family. She carries its destinies in the folds of her mantle.

Henri Amiel

Herbert Clark Hoover was only six when his father died; but before his mother passed away he was nearly ten, so that her sweetness and humility remained with him forever. In the four years of her widowhood Huldah Hoover supported her three children by taking in sewing, but her real vocation was preaching. Quakers throughout Iowa came to know her soft, unstudied eloquence. Though Herbert remembered few of her words, their general purport, which was love and charity, colored his mind and instincts indelibly.

Eugene Lyons

PORTRAIT OF MOTHER

Little Girls, it is said, are made of sugar and spice and everything nice. By the time all the sugar and spice has worn off, they become mothers and all they have left is everything nice, but that lasts forever.

Still they are all different. Some mothers are chubby while others are little wisps, thin as an April breeze. Some are freckled and husky. Some are loud and others are mousy. Some are Esquimaux, Democrats, secretaries, D. A. R.s, factory workers, Sioux, socialites, and Red Cross ladies, but mostly they are just mothers with husbands to clean up after, children to love and to spank, and houses to turn into homes.

Mothers are the people who sweep out the mountain cabins, run the carpet sweepers in Centerville, plug in the vacuum cleaners in Cedar Rapids, and see that the maids tidy up the apartments on Fifth Avenue. Mothers cook, clean, wash, mend, dream, punish, wheedle, improvise, cajole, and make things go twice as far as a man ever could. Children are what they read to, listen for, play with, watch over, think about, pray for, worry with, do without because of, and brag to the neighbors about. A bobby pin and gummed tape are Mother's kit of tools; intuition is her college degree; and a new hat is her Declaration of Independence.

All mothers, from the Arctic Circle to the Equator, have the reputation of being wonderful cooks. The older we become and the farther we wander, the more we are convinced that nobody anywhere can make quite as good an apple pie (or jerked walrus goulash) as Mother. Dear old

Mother — was she really the cook we thought her to be back in the days when our cast-iron stomachs could digest anything we could chew up?

Mothers are patient souls. Your mother, in particular, must have been a blue ribbon patience winner when you were young. How else could she have raised such a one as you? Patience alone couldn't have done it; it took many cubic miles of love and lucky for you (lucky for all of us) that a mother's heart is as boundless as the universe itself. Anyone else would have scrubbed our ears, dressed us in our Sunday best, and sent us packing to the nearest orphans' home after the first two or three years of trying to convert a small savage into a civilized boy or girl.

When we were little, Mother was everything to us — the police department, the board of education, the department of public works, the recreation commission, the finance department, the court of correction. She was a busy person. The only reason she wasn't driven out of her mind is because she was a mother with the leadership of Moses, the courage of Daniel, and the patience of Job.

All mothers are beautiful when they are young — remember? Then as the years turn into decades, Mother meets another man besides Dad and this man is Old Father Time. Her fresh beauty changes after she and Old Father Time get to be good friends. There are little cut lines on her thumb made by the paring knife and the winter winds roughen her cheeks when she hangs out the clothes (even when she uses all those magic creams). She doesn't carry the grocery bags so jauntily as when you were skipping along by her side. And her eyes, once dancing, are tired because they have seen so many, many things. Then one day, Mother looks in the mirror and says to herself, "I am no longer pretty," and it is a sad and lonely day. Mother is seldom wrong, but she was wrong that time. The beauty of mothers is as indestructible as Faith, Hope, and Love because mothers are all these things and more.

When the years roll on and the children scatter to the faraway places of the earth, Mother's job is done. Her little ones have become young men and women, for better or for worse, and there is nothing left that she can possibly do. Now she can sit back and relax and take things easy in the golden autumn of her life. But does she? No! Now she has grandchildren to visit, to plan for, to buy for, to make for, to sew for, to knit for, and if she lives long enough she becomes a great-grand-mother. Only then can she stop and rest and spend the remainder of her days just being as beautiful as only great-grandmothers can be.

But whether she be eighteen or eighty, Mother is an irreplaceable treasure. None other will ever love you half so well or half so foolishly. None other will be so sure you are right, good and worthy. Of course, sometimes she is wrong, but God love her for it and keep her forever in His grace.

Alan Beck

Where We Love, Is Home

Home, that our feet may leave, but not our hearts.

Oliver Wendell Holmes

Only Heaven Is Given Away

I bought a gay-roofed house upon a sunny hill,
Where heaven is very close to earth and all the
    world is still.
It took my savings, every cent, although the cost
    was small,
But, oh, the lovely things I bought, and paid for
    not at all!
The sleepy valleys that below in tawny sunshine
    lie,
The oaks that sprawl across their slopes and
    climb to meet the sky,
Stray winds that sing of other things than
    those our eyes may see,
Blue wisps of mist, and reveled clouds that,
    fleeing, beckon me.

White suns of mad, glad April, October's
    wine to quaff,
On crystal winter mornings my hearth fire's
    crackling laugh,
The silent stars that march at night so close
    above my head,
The sound of raindrops on the roof when I am
    snug in bed.
For joist and beam and shingles gay I spent
    my savings small,
But on the lovely things God gave, He put no
    price at all.

Rose Darrough

A house is built of logs and stone,
    Of tiles and posts and piers;
A home is built of loving deeds
    That stand a thousand years.

Victor Hugo

I want to thank Thee, Father,
For the fragrances of home;
The spiciness of gingerbread,
The sunny smell of clothes just off the line,
The children's hair
Clean from fresh shampooing,
The coziness of moth balls
As the winter clothes
Are taken from their trunks.

And let me not forget
Spring coming in the window
As I make the beds,
Nor the heavenly fragrance
Of the baby's neck.

Myra Scovel

THE HOUSE BEAUTIFUL

The Crown of the house is Godliness
The Beauty of the house is Order
The Glory of the house is Hospitality
The Blessing of the house is Contentment

Old Inscription

As the homes, so the state.

A. Bronson Alcott

Because I have been sheltered, fed,
By thy good care,
I cannot see another's lack
And I not share
My glowing fire, my loaf of bread,
My roof's safe shelter overhead,
That he, too, may be comforted.

Grace Noll Crowell

LIKE MOTHER USED TO MAKE

The other day, I read in a readers'-request column this plea: "Can someone please tell me how to make old-fashioned apple strudel? I have the recipe my mother used; but somehow, my apple strudel never turns out the way hers did, and I'm wondering what I could be doing wrong."

Will she ever find the secret? I, too, wondered. No matter how many readers try to help her, how many suggestions she receives about the extra dash of sugar, the freshness of the butter, the temperature of the oven, the timing of the baking, will any one ever be able to reproduce the magic formula that was her mother's, and hers alone?

Like Mother used to make . . . Bakers long have claimed the slogan; advertisers have lured us with it to their pickles and catsups and jellies and jams.

Like Mother used to make . . . The very words conjure up a kitchen where a woman toils lovingly to fashion her family's favorite dishes. It paints a nostalgic picture of children flocking around wanting to help — to beat the eggs, to stir the batter, to roll out the piecrust, to cut the cookies, to handle the bread dough. It re-creates a hundred small, significant scenes — of people who come sniffing into a kitchen, begging a taste of this, a nibble of that, peering into the oven and pleading, "Something smells good. Is supper ready? I'm starved."

Like Mother used to make . . . The cheese soufflé. The nut bread. The chicken casserole. The potato pancakes. The cherry pie. The Christmas plum pudding.

Recipes we have aplenty, passed along to daughters, presented to sons' brides. "Johnny is awfully fond of upside-down cake. I always made it this way." And eagerly the young wife follows directions, does her best to duplicate that special dish. But she knows, even when he's too polite to tell her, that something is different about it. Whatever her skills or practice, something is missing, some rare, lost ingredient that not even the best-intentioned cook can supply.

Because a mother stirs a little bit of herself into everything she cooks for her family. Unseen, all unsuspected, into the bowl goes the subtle flavor of her personality — the way she thinks and feels, the way she laughs or tilts her head or scolds. And into this dish of hers, too, go the whole measure and taste of the home — the way the dining room used to look when the lamps were lighted, the sound of family voices, the laughter, the quarrels, the memories.

These are the ingredients we lack when we try to reproduce the dish that Mother used to make. These are her secret spices. They are not for sale, and they can't be passed along.

Yet every woman who enters a kitchen carries with her a rare and precious store of her own. The flavor of *herself* in relation to her children; the warmth and tang and savor of her own household. Daily, inescapably, without ever realizing it, all of us are blending these inimitable components into other dishes, into other lives.

So that one day our children, too, will say, "My mother used to make the most wonderful peach cobbler. I simply can't make it come out the same, no matter how hard I try!"

Marjorie Holmes

But what on earth is half so dear —
So longed for — as the hearth of home?

Emily Brontë

Stay, stay at home, my heart, and rest;
Home-keeping hearts are happiest.

Henry Wadsworth Longfellow

HOUSE BLESSING

Bless the four corners of this house,
And be the lintel blest.
And bless the hearth, and bless the board,
And bless each place of rest.
And bless the door that opens wide
To strangers as to kin,
And bless each crystal window pane
That lets the sunshine in,
And bless the rooftree overhead
And every sturdy wall.
The peace of man, the peace of God
The peace of love on all.

Arthur Guiterman

He is happiest, be he king or peasant, who finds
his peace in his home.

Goethe

God bless our home, and help us
    To love each other true;
To make our home the kind of place
    Where everything we do
Is filled with love and kindness,
    A dwelling place for Thee,
And help us, God, each moment,
    To live most helpfully.

KITCHEN PRAYER

Lord of all pots and pans, and things,
Since I've not time to be
A saint by doing lovely things
Or watching late with Thee,
Or dreaming in the dawn light,
Or storming heaven's gates,
Make me a saint by getting meals
And washing up the plates.

Warm all the kitchen with Thy love
And light it with Thy peace.
Forgive me all my worry,
And make my grumbling cease.
Thou who didst love to give men food,
In room or by the sea,
Accept the service that I do.
I do it unto Thee.

M. K. H.

I can still smell the warm spicy smells of ginger-snaps baking in the oven, of apple pies rich with cinnamon, and of countless doughnuts merrily bobbing about on the surface of boiling fat. My mother sang hymns as she went about her work and often encouraged us to sing with her. One of her favorites was "Shall we gather at the River?" and all of us, joining in the chorus, loved to assure her that we would most certainly gather there. "Yes, we'll gather at the river, the beautiful river, the beautiful river," we would all shout together, each, I feel sure, thinking of that river only as some pleasant family picnicking ground on some pleasant undefined day in the future.

Mary Ellen Chase

"THE FRENCH CHEF"

The TV camera zooms in for a close-up (of Julia Child) and focuses on her hands. She may be dicing an onion, mincing a garlic clove, trussing a chicken. Her fingers fly with the speed and dexterity of a concert pianist. Strength counts, too, as she cleaves an ocean catfish with a mighty, two-fisted swipe or, muscles bulging and curls aquiver, whips up egg whites with her wire whisk. She takes every shortcut, squeezes lemons through "my ever-clean dish towel," samples sauces with her fingers. No matter if she breaks the rules; her verve and insouciance will see her through. Even her *faux pas* are classic. When a potato pancake falls on the worktable, she scoops it back into the pan, bats her big blue eyes at the cameras and advises, "Remember, you're all alone in the kitchen and no one can see you."

From *Time*

There is no spectacle on earth more appealing than that of a woman in the act of cooking dinner for someone she loves.

Thomas Wolfe

TENTING TONIGHT

A man and his young son went on a camping trip without Mother. After one night in the woods, the father asked his son how he was enjoying outdoor life. "Fine, Dad," said the boy. "But next time, let's bring Mamma and the catsup."

Baltimore Sunday Sun

RED GERANIUMS

Life did not bring me silken gowns,
Nor jewels for my hair,
Nor sight of gabled, foreign towns
In distant countries fair.
But I can glimpse, beyond my pane,
    a green and friendly hill,
And red geraniums aflame, upon
    my window-sill.

Martha Haskell Clark

A hundred men can make an encampment, but
it requires a woman to make a home.

WHAT IS CHARM?

Charm is the measure of attraction's power
To chain the fleeting fancy of an hour
And rival all the spell of Beauty's dower.

A subtle grace of heart and mind that flows
With tactful sympathy; the sweetest rose,
If not the fairest, that the garden knows.

A quick responsiveness in word and deed,
A dignity and stateliness at need,
The will to follow or the art to lead.

She to whom this most gracious gift is known
Has life's great potent factor for her own,
And rules alike the cottage and the throne.

Louisa Carroll Thomas

My Home Is Hallowed Ground to Me

My home to me is hallowed ground
Where Paradise on earth is found.
Ardor and faith and joy divine
I pour into this task of mine . . .

To make the home a place of joys,
To bless and guide my girls and boys,
Be inspiration, helper, friend,
To him whose fate with mine must blend —
What holier mission could there be?
My home is hallowed ground to me.

To be popular at home is a great achievement. The man who is loved by the house cat, by the dog, by the neighbor's children, and by his own wife, is a great man, even if he has never had his name in Who's Who.

Thomas Dreier

When true love has found a home, every new year forms one more ring around the hearts of those who love each other, so that in the end they cannot live apart.

Julius Stinde

Love is patient: Love is kind and envies no one.
Love is never boastful, nor conceited, nor rude;
Never selfish, not quick to take offense.
Keeps no score of wrongs; does not gloat
Over other men's sins, but delights in the truth.
There is nothing love cannot face; there is no limit
To its faith, its hope, and its endurance.

I Corinthians 13: 4-7
New English Bible

Sweet is the smile of home; the mutual look
When hearts are of each other sure.

John Keble

Whom God loves, his house is sweet to him.

Cervantes

A little house well fill'd,
A little land well till'd,
And a little wife well will'd
Are great riches.

English Proverb

The Heart Goes Home

Always the heart goes home on Christmas Eve . . .
Goes silently across a continent,
Or mountains or the sea. A heart will leave
The glitter of a city street, and sent
By something deep and timeless, find the way
To a little cottage on a country hill.

And even if the little cottage may
Have disappeared, a heart will find it still . . .

The smile of tenderness upon the faces,
The simple words, the arms secure and strong,
The sweetness of the well-remembered places . . .

All these a heart will find and will belong
Once more to country hills, however far,
And sense the holy presence of the Star.

Grace V. Watkins

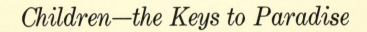

Children—the Keys to Paradise

Suffer the little children to come unto me, and forbid them not: for of such is the kingdom of God.

Mark 10: 14

Our children. Yet not ours,
They are their own
Whom no one can possess.
For all the future holds of good or ill
They are their own.
Unless, dear Lord, unless
By miracles of grace
And mercy infinite
They are possessed by Thee
And so become more their own
By being Thine.

Minton Johnston

A baby is God's opinion that the world should
go on.

Carl Sandburg

THE CHILD'S QUESTION

Will there really be a morning?
Is there such a thing as day?
Could I see it from the mountains
If I were as tall as they?

Has it feet like water-lilies?
Has it feathers like a bird?
Does it come from famous countries
Of which I have never heard?

Oh, some scholar, Oh, some sailor,
Oh, some wise man from the skies,
Please to tell a little pilgrim
Where the place called morning lies?

Emily Dickinson

WHAT A BABY COSTS

"How much do babies cost?" said he
The other night upon my knee;
And then I said: "They cost a lot;
A lot of watching by a cot,
A lot of sleepless hours and care,
A lot of heart-ache and despair,
A lot of fear and trying dread,
And sometimes many tears are shed
In payment for our babies small,
But every one is worth it all.

"For babies people have to pay
A heavy price from day to day —
There is no way to get one cheap.
Why, sometimes when they're fast asleep
You have to get up in the night
And go and see that they're all right.
But what they cost in constant care
And worry, does not half compare
With what they bring of joy and bliss —
You'd pay much more for just a kiss.

"Who buys a baby has to pay
A portion of the bill each day;
He has to give his time and thought
Unto the little one he's bought.
He has to stand a lot of pain
Inside his heart and not complain;
And pay with lonely days and sad
For all the happy hours he's had.
All this a baby costs, and yet
His smile is worth it all, you bet."

Edgar A. Guest

Children are poor men's treasures.

Japanese Proverb

"Isn't there one child you really love the best?" a mother was asked. And she replied, "Yes. The one who is sick until he gets well; the one who's away, until he gets home."

Send Them to Bed with a Kiss

O mothers, so weary, discouraged,
    Worn out with the cares of the day,
You often grow cross and impatient,
    Complain of the noise and the play;
For the day brings so many vexations,
    So many things going amiss;
But, mothers, whatever may vex you,
    Send the children to bed with a kiss!

The dear little feet wander often,
    Perhaps from the pathway of right,
The dear little hands find new mischief
    To try you from morning till night;
But think of the desolate mothers
    Who'd give all the world for your bliss,
And, as thanks for your infinite blessings,
    Send the children to bed with a kiss!

For some day their noise will not vex you,
    The silence will hurt you far more;
You will long for their sweet childish voices,
    For a sweet childish face at the door;
And to press a child's face to your bosom,
    You'd give all the world for just this;
For the comfort 'twill bring you in sorrow,
    Send the children to bed with a kiss!

TO A DAUGHTER

You are the trip I did not take.
You are the pearls I cannot buy.
You are my blue Italian lake.
You are my piece of foreign sky.

Anne Campbell

Thou art thy mother's glass, and she in thee
Calls back the lovely April of her prime.

Shakespeare

LOSING BATTLE

This, I have learned,
Is children's technique:
They whittle you down
Till you're helplessly weak.
Then even the smallest,
Most innocent tyke,
Instinctively knowing
The moment, will strike.
So here is the sequence,
No parent can win:
First you give out,
And then you give in.

Richard Armour

A child should always say what's true
And speak when he is spoken to,
And behave mannerly at table;
At least as far as he is able.

Robert Louis Stevenson

"EVERY BOY SHOULD HAVE A DOG"

Every boy should have a dog.
I've had it drummed into my ears
continually for seven years.
Of course, a boy should have a dog.

I have succumbed to pleading eye,
to smudge of mud on quivering chin,
his hopeful father joining in
to tell again the reasons why.

And now I find this muff of joy
that chews his shoes, that licks his face,
has proved beyond the slightest trace
that every dog should have a boy.

Myra Scovel

SPRING MUDITATION

Who could punish a little boy
When he comes in muddy from head to feet,
His freckles ruddy from the wind,
His smile angelical and sweet?

Knowing the fun of sailing boats
In shiny puddles, who could scold
And put one cloud in the new spring sky
Of a happy lad, just six years old?

Though he tracked his mud from room to room,
Who could take him across her knee
And firmly spank his soggy pants?
Me!

Beulah Fenderson Smith

THE VELVET HAND

I call that parent rash and wild
Who'd reason with a six-year child,
Believing little twigs are bent
By calm, considered argument.

In bandying words with progeny,
There's no percentage I can see,
And people who, imprudent, do so,
Will wonder how their troubles grew so.

Now underneath this tranquil roof
Where sounder theories have their proof,
Our life is sweet, our infants happy.
In quietude dwell Mammy and Pappy.

We've sworn a stern, parental vow
That argument we won't allow.
Brooking no juvenile excess here,
We say a simple No or Yes, here,
And then, when childish wails begin

We don't debate.
We just give in.

Phyllis McGinley

ON THE RUN

When children are small
They run up stairs,
They run up walks,
They race in pairs.

They run up ramps,
They run up hills;
Then a few years later
They run up bills.

Richard Armour

Prayer at a Nursery Window

So brief a time I have them, Lord,
To steady them with Thy bright word;
A narrow span of childish days
To set their feet in Thy green ways —
A few swift nights to know them warm,
Close-gathered now from any harm,
Looming in shadowy years ahead . . .
How can I help but be afraid?

The little wisdom I have won
Is not enough to guard my son.
The grace I grope for, deed by deed,
Cannot assuage my daughter's need;
Nor wit, nor courage hold at bay
The moment, that imperiled day,
For which no foresight may prepare —
Not even love, not even prayer.

Be to them, God, all I would be
In that far time I shall not see;
And guide me now, their friend, their mother,
To hear their prayers, to smooth the cover,
And leave their window wide upthrust
Beneath that Heaven of my trust,
Whose pity marked a sparrow's fall
And bends in mercy over all.

Frances Stoakley Lankford

The mother's heart is the child's schoolroom.

Henry Ward Beecher

Soft is the heart of a child; do not harden it.

To My Son

I will not say to you, "This is the way; walk in it."
For I do not know your way or where the Spirit
    may call you.
It may be to paths I have never trod or ships on
    the sea leading to unimagined lands afar,
Or haply, to a star!

Or yet again
Through dark and perilous places racked with
    pain and full of fear
Your road may lead you far away from me
    or near —
I cannot guess or guide, but only stand aside.

Just this I say:
I know for every truth there is a way for each
    to walk, a right for each to choose, a truth to use.
And though you wander far, your soul will know
    that true path when you find it.

Therefore, go!
I will fear nothing for you day or night!
I will not grieve at all because your light is
    called by some new name;
Truth is the same!
It matters nothing to call it star or sun —
All light is one.

Children need models more than they need
critics.

Joseph Joubert

The best way to make children good is to make
them happy.

Oscar Wilde

FIRST HAIRCUT

The barber pins the towel around his neck;
His mother murmurs, ". . . first time . . . I don't
    know
Just how he'll act . . ." The barber nods. He asks,
"Want to hear the little airplane go?"

This is no airplane, not this angry thing
That creeps along his neck and past his ears,
And gnaws with tingling teeth into his hair.
He protests louder when he feels the shears
That snap and bite above his helpless wail,
And leave his innocent small head forlorn.
His mother sooths him, "No tears — big boy now!"
He somehow knows his Samson strength is shorn.

Now at last the long ordeal is through.
He has joined the manner of his kind.
The barber lifts him down — "You're all boy now!"
He smiles through his late tears; while newly
    blind,
His mother slips one clipped curl from the floor,
Then takes her sudden-stranger through the door.

Edna Casler Joll

We used to wash his hands for him,
But, now that he is not so small,
He scrubs his own, unhelped, while we
Just wash the sink, the soap, the wall.

Luke Neely

The only thing that children wear out faster
than shoes are parents and teachers.

EVERY CHILD

Every child should know a hill,
And the clean joy of running down
    its long slope
With the wind in his hair.
He should know a tree —
The comfort of its cool lap of shade,
And the supple strength of its arms
Balancing him between earth and sky
So he is creature of both.
He should know some bit of singing water —
The strange mysteries in its depths,
And the long sweet grasses that border it.

Every child should know some scrap
Of uninterrupted sky, to shout against;
And have one star, dependable and bright,
For wishing on.

Edna Casler Joll

INTERRUPTION

How can I write a poem
with you two there at the door,
watching me every moment,
asking questions galore?

Do you remember the artist,
Raphael was his name,
who painted as cherubs the urchins
who played at his window frame?

Now if you two are determined
to keep running in all the time,
you *may* find yourselves, my darlings,
with your heads sticking out of a rhyme.

Myra Scovel

Reasoning with a child is fine, if you can reach
the child's reason without destroying your own.

John Mason Brown

ONE CROWDED HOUR OF GLORIOUS STRIFE

I love my daughters with a love unfailing,
I love them healthy and I love them ailing.
I love them as sheep are loved by the shepherd,
With a fiery love like a lion or a leopard.
I love them gentle or inclined to mayhem —
But I love them warmest after eight-thirty a.m.

Oh, the peace like heaven
    That wraps me around,
Say, at eight-thirty — seven,
    When they're schoolroom-bound
With the last glove mated
    And the last scarf tied,
With the pigtail plaited,
    With the pincurl dried,
And the egg disparaged,
    And the porridge sneered at,
And last night's comics furtively peered at,
The coat apprehended
    On its ultimate hook,
And the cover mended
    On the history book!

How affection swells, how my heart leaps up
As I sip my coffee from a lonely cup!
For placid as the purling of woodland waters
Is a house divested of its morning daughters.
Sweeter than the song of the lark in the sky
Are my darlings' voices as they shriek good-by —

With the last shoe burnished
  And the last pen filled,
And the bus fare furnished
  And the radio stilled;
When I've signed the excuses
  And written the notes,
And poured fresh juices
  Down ritual throats,
And rummaged for umbrellas
  Lest the day grow damper,
And rescued homework from an upstairs
  hamper,
And stripped my wallet
  In the daily shakedown,
And tottered to my pallet
For a nervous breakdown.

Oh, I love my daughters with a love that's
  reckless
As Cornelia's for the jewels in her fabled
  necklace.
But Cornelia, even, must have raised three cheers
At the front door closing on her school-bent dears.

Phyllis McGinley

In dealing with our children, we don't lean on
any of the more advanced methods of child psy-
chology. I tend to remember the immortal words
of that philosopher and father, Moss Hart, who
once announced that in dealing with *his* children
he kept one thing in mind: "We're bigger than
they are, and it's *our* house."

Jean Kerr

The opinions expressed by this child are not
necessarily those of his mother.

Note to teacher on child's first day at school

To the First-Grade Teacher

To your clean hands I now commend
This child with lipstick kiss on ear —
And hope you find him such a friend
As I, who kept him awfully near.

He knows so little — Teddy bears,
And white-railed bed, and cooky jars,
And yet is wondering about
The rest — including seas and stars.

And now it comes — the words, the books,
And what "goes into," adds and "borrows" —
I will take care of his today —
You, his tomorrows.

Elizabeth Henley

Dear God, what could be sweeter
Than this pile of baby clothes!
Cream woolly shirts like golden fleece,
Soft muslins edged with shells of lace,
Pink sweaters with their bonnets
Round, to frame a baby face.
The finely woven blankets
That are meant for cuddling,
And Grandma's cashmere double gown
Feather-stitched with love.

Myra Scovel

With one child you may walk,
With two you may ride,
But when you have three,
At home you must bide.

Cornish Proverb

Sometimes, looking deep into the eyes of a child, you are conscious of meeting a glance full of wisdom. The child has known nothing yet but love and beauty — all this piled-up world knowledge you have acquired is unguessed at by him. And yet you meet this wonderful look that tells you in a moment more than all the years of experience have seemed to teach.

Hildegarde Hawthorne

AFTER SCHOOL

A house should have a cookie jar,
For when it's half-past three,
And children hurry home from school
As hungry as can be,
There's nothing quite so splendid
In filling children up,
As spicy, fluffy ginger cakes,
And sweet milk in a cup.

A house should have a mother
Waiting with a hug,
No matter what a boy brings home,
A puppy or a bug.
For children only loiter
When the bell rings to dismiss,
If no one's home to greet them
With a cookie or a kiss!

Helen Welshimer

TEN, GOING ON ELEVEN

He is working hard on his stamp collection;
He is saving clarinet reeds,
And random rocks for their shapes or color,
And watermelon seeds.

There are seventeen white mice in his dresser
And eleven turtles on top —
I hope, when it's time to think about girls,
His collecting spirit will stop.

Lois Leurgans

TO A TWELVE YEAR OLD

Tell me what you're thinking of —
Priam's war, the new pet dove,
how to make a tractor go,
the guy in last night's movie show?

Are you miles and miles away
holding court in old Pompeii,
or are you somewhat nearer home,
flying from the court house dome?

Perhaps you're someone very great
whose word decides a nation's fate.
I'd like so much to catch your eye;
I've said three times, "Please pass the pie."

Myra Scovel

"Mother," asked a little girl out of a sudden silence, "when will I be old enough to wear the kind of shoes that kill you?"

I have found the best way to give advice to young children is to find out what they want and then advise them to do it.

Harry S. Truman

And when with envy time transported,
  Shall think to rob us of our joys,

You'll in your girls again be courted,
  And I'll go wooing in my boys.

Gilbert Cooper

There's only one pretty child in the world, and every mother has it.

Cheshire Proverb

RECIPE FOR PRESERVING CHILDREN

1 large grassy field
3 children
2 small dogs
A brook with pebbles
A hot sun
A deep blue sky
A summer day

Mix children with dogs, blend with sunshine, empty into field, and stir continuously. Pour brook gently over pebbles. Sprinkle field with flowers. Cover all with deep blue sky and bake in hot sun.

When children are well browned, call them home. Will be found ready to take from the oven and cool in bath tub.

Delicious when served with love and kisses.

Prayer—the Soul's Sincere Desire

Pray without ceasing. In everything give thanks: for this is the will of God in Christ Jesus concerning you.

I Thessalonians 5: 17-18

What Is Prayer?

Prayer is the soul's sincere desire,
    Uttered or unexpressed —
The motion of a hidden fire,
    That kindles in the breast.

Prayer is the burthen of a sigh,
    The falling of a tear —
The upward glancing of an eye,
    When none but God is near.

Prayer is the simplest form of speech
    That infant lips can try —
Prayer the sublimest strains that reach
    The majesty on high.

         *   *   *

O Thou by whom we come to God —
    The Life, the Truth, the Way!
The path of prayer Thyself hast trod;
    Lord, teach us how to pray.

James Montgomery

I remember my mother's prayers — and they have always followed me. They have clung to me all my life.

Abraham Lincoln

God grant me the serenity
to accept things I cannot change,
Courage to change things I can,
and wisdom to know the difference.

Reinhold Niebuhr

MY PRAYER

Please help me, Lord, to cherish sacred things:
Help me to keep a child's deep trust in me,
Teach me to listen when a robin sings,
To watch a spider weave its artistry.

Give me the keys that will unlock the hearts
Of all I meet; please help me understand
Ways not my own that fill their daily charts,
Encourage me to offer them my hand.

Show me the grace of sparrows in the snow,
Help me to teach my children gold is cold,
That what can be replaced has little glow
And only gentle deeds wear well when old;

Remind me, Peace will be a dream come true,
When men follow the Star that leads to You.

Annette Victorin

God, our Heavenly Father, we draw near to Thee with thankful hearts because of all Thy great love for us. We thank Thee most of all for the gift of Thy dear son, in whom alone we may be one. We are different from one another in race and language, in material things, in gifts, in opportunities, but each of us has a woman's heart, knowing joy and sorrow, pleasure and pain. We are one in our need of Thy forgiveness, Thy strength, Thy love; make us one in our common response to Thee, that bound by a common love and freed from selfish aims we may work for the good of all and the advancement of Thy Kingdom. Through Jesus Christ, our Lord.

Queen Salote, The Tonga Islands

Prayer for My Sixteen Year Old Daughter

She is sixteen and beautiful as dawn!
I make no prayer to stay her hour of living;
O Father, this I cannot ask of you;
To spare her loss and pain and joy of giving,
To hold the petaled bud, the drop of dew,
And keep her with eternal youth
And days that weave a careless fantasy.
I would not rob her of the thorns of truth
For sorrow deeply pays for ecstasy.

I do not pray that early love be kind to her.
I know how lesser loves prepare
The youthful heart and discipline the mind
For one great love the heavens lean to share.

Just this I ask to be retained complete,
This bit of youth when years have made her wise;
O Father, let no earthly thing defeat
The eagerness for life within her eyes.

Dorothy Callaway

Billy (Graham's) Mother, soon after his conversion, set aside a period every day for prayer devoted solely to Billy and the "calling" she believed was his. She continued those prayers, never missing a day, for seven years until the last uncertainty was resolved and Billy was well on his preaching way. She still continues them, though now her prayer — with a text drawn from II Timothy 2: 15 — is that what he preaches may meet with God's approval: "Study to shew thyself approved unto God, a workman that needeth not to be ashamed, rightly dividing the word of truth."

Stanley High

A Woman's Prayer

O Lord, who knowest every need of mine,
Help me to bear each cross and not repine;
Grant me fresh courage every day,
Help me to do my work alway
    Without complaint!

O Lord, Thou knowest well how dark the way,
Guide Thou my footsteps, lest they stray;
Give me fresh faith for every hour,
Lest I should ever doubt Thy power
    And make complaint!

Give me a heart, O Lord, strong to endure,
Help me to keep it simple, pure,
Make me unselfish, helpful, true
In every act, whate'er I do,
    And keep content.

Help me to do my woman's share,
Make me courageous, strong to bear
Sunshine or shadow in my life!
Sustain me in the daily strife
    To keep content!

Our Creator would never have made such lovely
days, and have given us the deep hearts to enjoy
them above and beyond all that, unless we were
meant to be immortal.

Nathaniel Hawthorne

Between the humble and contrite heart and the
majesty of heaven there are no barriers; the only
password is prayer.

Hosea Ballou

THE MOTHER'S HYMN

Lord, who ordainest for mankind
    Benignant toils and tender cares,
We thank Thee for the ties that bind
    The mother to the child she bears.

We thank Thee for the hopes that rise
    Within her heart, as, day by day,
The dawning soul, from those young eyes,
    Looks with a clearer, steadier ray.

And grateful for the blessing given
    With that dear infant on her knee,
She trains the eye to look to heaven,
    The voice to lisp a prayer to Thee.

Such thanks the blessed Mary gave
    When from her lap the Holy Child,
Sent from on high to seek and save
    The lost of earth, looked up and smiled.

All-Gracious! grant to those who bear
    A mother's charge, the strength and light
To guide the feet that own their care
    In ways of Love and Truth and Right.

William Cullen Bryant

BENEDICTION

The Lord bless thee, and keep thee:
The Lord make his face shine upon thee,
And be gracious unto thee:
The Lord lift up his countenance upon thee
And give thee peace.

Numbers 6: 24-26

ACKNOWLEDGMENTS

The compiler and the publisher gratefully acknowledge the per-mission of the following publishers and copyright owners for the use of the protected material indicated:

ABINGDON PRESS for permission to reprint "Spring Muditation" by Beulah Fenderson Smith, from *Together* Magazine, March 1967, copyright © 1967 by The Methodist Publishing House.

RICHARD ARMOUR and GOOD HOUSEKEEPING MAGAZINE for "Losing Battle" by Richard Armour. Reprinted by permission from the September, 1967, issue of *Good House-keeping* Magazine, © 1967 by the Hearst Corporation; and by permission of the author, Richard Armour.

RICHARD ARMOUR for permission to reprint the poem, "On the Run" by Richard Armour.

THE ASSOCIATED PRESS for permission to reprint the syndicated column, "Dear Mom: ..." by Hal (Harold V.) Boyle from The *New York World-Telegram and Sun*, May 12, 1956, copyright 1956 by The Associated Press.

THE BALTIMORE SUN for "Tenting Tonight" which appeared originally in the *Baltimore Sunday Sun.*

JACOB M. BRAUDE for permission to reprint "What Is a Mother?" by William A. Greenebaum II from the *Second Encyclopedia of Stories, Quotations and Anecdotes* compiled and edited by Jacob M. Braude, copyright 1957 by Prentice-Hall, Inc.

JOHN MASON BROWN for permission to reprint a specified selection, "Reasoning with a child is fine ..."

HUGH BURR and THE CURTIS PUBLISHING COMPANY for "We used to wash his hands for him ..." by Luke Neely, which first appeared in *The Saturday Evening Post*, copyright 1957 by The Curtis Publishing Company. Reprinted by permission of Hugh Burr.

CAMBRIDGE UNIVERSITY PRESS for permission to use the passage from I Corinthians 13:4-7 from *The New English Bible, New Testament*, © The Delegates of the Oxford University Press and the Syndics of the Cambridge University Press, 1961. Reprinted by permission of The Cambridge University Press.

AL CAPP for "Mother and Her Secret," condensed from *Monitor*, an NBC-Radio Broadcast, copyright 1964 by Al Capp. Reprinted by permission of Mr. Capp.

THE CATHOLIC POETRY SOCIETY OF AMERICA for "At a Nursery Window" by Frances Stoakley Lankford, from *Spirit*, copyrighted by The Catholic Poetry Society of America.

CBS TELEVISION NETWORK for a specified selection from the *Person to Person* Series, broadcast on May 27, 1955.

THE CURTIS PUBLISHING COMPANY for "What Is a Mother?" by Nan Carroll. Re-printed with permission from *Ladies Home Journal* © 1956 by The Curtis Publishing Company.

DODD, MEAD & COMPANY for permission to reprint "How We Kept Mother's Day" from *Laugh With Leacock* by Stephen Leacock, copyright © 1930 by Dodd, Mead & Company, Inc. copyright renewed: and a specified selection from *Our Hearts Were Young and Gay* by Cornelia Otis Skinner and Emily Kimbrough, copyright 1942 by Dodd, Mead & Company, Inc.

DOUBLEDAY & COMPANY for a specified selection from *Our Unknown Ex-President: A Portrait of Hoover* by Eugene Lyons, copyright 1948 by Doubleday & Company, Inc.; and for a specified selection from *Please Don't Eat the Daisies* by Jean Kerr, copy-right 1957 by Doubleday & Company, Inc. Both reprinted by permission of Doubleday & Company, Inc. Publishers.

E. P. DUTTON & COMPANY for "After School" from *Singing Drums* by Helen Welshimer, copyright, 1937, by Helen Welshimer; copyright renewal © 1965 by Ralph Welshimer. Reprinted by permission.

FUNK & WAGNALLS for permission to reprint two specified selections from *Mothers of Great Men and Women* by Laura C. Halloway, copyright 1883 by Funk & Wagnalls, Publishers.

MRS. ARTHUR GUITERMAN and HARPER & ROW, PUBLISHERS, INC., for "House Blessing" from *The Mirthful Lyre*, reprinted in part from various periodicals by Harper and Brothers, Inc., copyright, 1918. Used by permission of Mrs. Arthur Guiterman.

HARCOURT, BRACE & WORLD, INC. for permission to reprint "A mother is not a person to lean on ..." from *Her Son's Wife* by Dorothy Canfield Fisher, copyright © 1926 by Harcourt, Brace & World, Inc.

HARPER & ROW, PUBLISHERS, INC. for "Definition" from *Flame in the Wind* by Grace Noll Crowell, copyright 1930, 1934 by Harper and Brothers, Inc.; specified lines from "Because of Thy Great Bounty" from *Light of The Years* by Grace Noll Crowell, copy-right 1936 by Harper and Brothers, Inc., copyright renewed 1964 by Grace Noll Crowell; and eight lines from Volume 2 *Selected Literary and Political Papers and Addresses of Woodrow Wilson*, copyright 1926 by Edith Bolling Wilson, Harper and Brothers, Publishers, Inc. All reprinted by permission of Harper & Row, Publishers, Inc.

ELIZABETH HENLEY and THE CURTIS PUBLISHING COMPANY for permission to reprint